DISCOVER THE MOST AMAZING AUTOMOBILES ON EARTH!

MEGA BOOK OF

CARS

Chrysalis Children's Books

INTERNET SAFETY

Always follow these guidelines for a fun and safe
journey through cyberspace:

1. Ask your parents for permission before you go online.

2. Spend time with your parents online
and show them your favorite sites.

3. Post your family's e-mail address, even if you have your
own (only give your personal address to someone you trust).

4. Do not reply to e-mails if you feel
they are strange or upsetting.

5. Do not use your real family name while you are online.

6. Never arrange to meet "cyber friends" in person
without your parents' permission.

7. Never give out your password.

8. Never give out your home address or telephone number.

9. Do not send scanned pictures of yourself
unless your parents approve.

10. Leave a website straight away if you find something that
is offensive or upsetting. Talk to your parents about it.

Every effort has been made to ensure none of the recommended websites in this book are linked to inappropriate material. However, due to the ever-changing nature of the Internet, the publishers regret they cannot take responsibility for future content of these websites. Therefore, it is strongly advised that children and parents consider the safety guidelines above.

First published in the UK in 2002
by Chrysalis Children's Books
an imprint of Chrysalis Books Group Plc
The Chrysalis Building, Bramley Road, London, W10 6SP
This paperback edition first published in 2005
www.chrysalisbooks.co.uk
Copyright © Chrysalis Children's Books 2002

Managing Editor: Nichola Tyrell
Art Director: Simon Rosenheim
Assistant Editor: Clare Chambers
Assistant Designer: Zeta Jones
Picture Researcher: Terry Forshaw

A CIP catalogue record for this book is available from the British Library.

ISBN 1 903954 06 1 (hb)
ISBN 1 84458 431 3 (pb)

Printed and bound in China.

This book can be ordered direct from the publisher.
Please contact the Marketing Department. But try your bookshop first.

CONTENTS

THE CAR CLOSE-UP

Since they were invented in the late 1800s, cars have developed at an incredible rate. Some models are not only a means of transportation, they're practically works of art! On the following pages you'll discover the fastest, the strangest, the most amazing cars of all time. Read about the history of the car and why some become classics. See the cars your parents might have driven in the 1970s – and what you might be driving in the 21st century! But first, how do these things work?

MEGA CRAWL
There are millions of cars in the world today, so it's no surprise that the roads are over-crowded. In some large cities, the average speed of traffic is the same as it was when we used horse-drawn carriages to get around!

Power steering makes manoeuvring easier when driving slowly or turning in small spaces.

POWER SOURCES

Before engines were invented, nature was the only source of power available. Animals pulled carts, and the earliest machines used wind or water power. Then came the steam engine, followed by the internal combustion engine in 1860, which revolutionised our lives. Most cars today use a four-stroke combustion cycle, known as the four-cycle engine, to convert petrol into motion.

There are two types of hydraulic brake systems used on cars — drum and disc. Most cars, like this 1992 Porsche Carrera, have discs at the front and drums at the rear.

How a four-cycle engine works

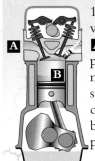

1. The intake valve opens **A** and the piston **B** moves down so the engine can take in both air and petrol.

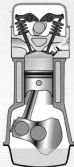

2. Then the piston moves back up and the mixture is squashed. This is called 'compression'.

3. A spark from a spark plug **C** makes this mixture explode. This is called 'combustion'.

4. The explosion pushes the piston down and waste gases out through the exhaust valve **D**.

Shock absorbers are part of the suspension system, and contribute to a smoother ride.

INTERNET LINK
http://www.brainpop.com/tech/transportation
Go to the Car page and check out the cartoon about engines, then build your own model with Bob the Rat!

Some cars, including this Porsche Carrera, have the engine at the rear of the body rather than the front.

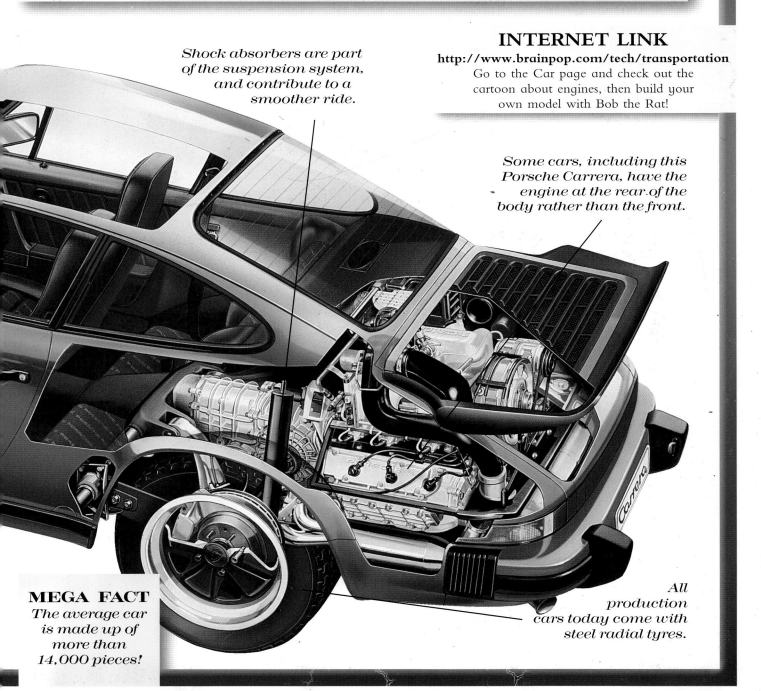

MEGA FACT
The average car is made up of more than 14,000 pieces!

All production cars today come with steel radial tyres.

FIRST ON FOUR WHEELS

The first car-like vehicle, the horseless carriage, was designed by Karl Benz and was on the road as early as 1886. Other budding designers soon followed his lead, including Henry Ford with his famous Model T (shown below). With the rapid advancement of the combustion engine, it was only a matter of time before Ford's dream became reality – and motor cars were everywhere!

TIN LIZZY INTERNATIONAL

The first Model T Ford was assembled near Detroit, Michigan, USA. But although Detroit produced the majority of Model Ts (or 'Tin Lizzies' as they became known), many were built in other countries such as Canada and England.

"YOU CAN PAINT IT ANY COLOUR... AS LONG AS IT'S BLACK!"

Although there is no proof that Henry Ford actually spoke these words, the phrase has always been linked with his name, and has survived for almost a century.

MODEL T MILLIONS

Between 1908 and 1927, Ford built a staggering 15 million cars with the Model T engine. Apart from the modern-day Volkswagen Beetle, this is the longest run of any single model in history!

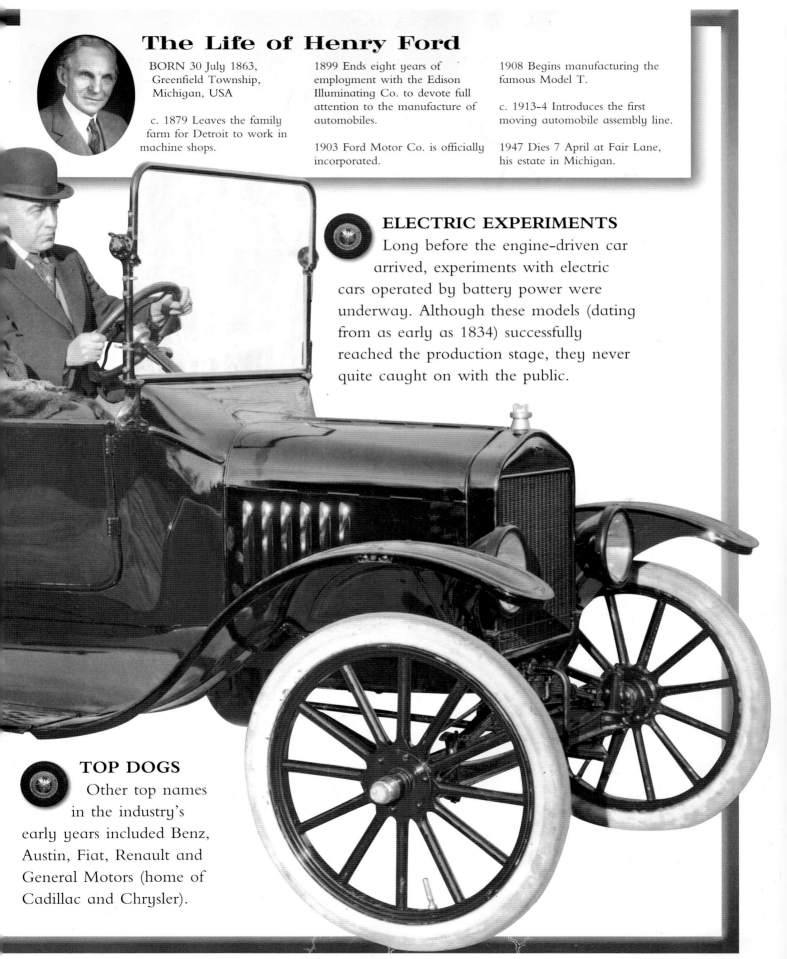

The Life of Henry Ford

BORN 30 July 1863, Greenfield Township, Michigan, USA

c. 1879 Leaves the family farm for Detroit to work in machine shops.

1899 Ends eight years of employment with the Edison Illuminating Co. to devote full attention to the manufacture of automobiles.

1903 Ford Motor Co. is officially incorporated.

1908 Begins manufacturing the famous Model T.

c. 1913-4 Introduces the first moving automobile assembly line.

1947 Dies 7 April at Fair Lane, his estate in Michigan.

ELECTRIC EXPERIMENTS

Long before the engine-driven car arrived, experiments with electric cars operated by battery power were underway. Although these models (dating from as early as 1834) successfully reached the production stage, they never quite caught on with the public.

TOP DOGS

Other top names in the industry's early years included Benz, Austin, Fiat, Renault and General Motors (home of Cadillac and Chrysler).

MODEL T FORD

Over the years, a wide variety of bodies were available, including vans, closed cars and even truck versions. Special bodies and many other parts could be bought easily, so it was possible to convert a Model T car to anything from a taxi to a tractor! At first, Model Ts had oil lamps and needed to be hand cranked to start the engine, which was pretty hard work!

INTERNET LINKS
http://www.modelt.org/kid1.html
Kids' section of the Model T Ford
Club's official website.
http://www.ipl.org:2000/autou
Take a tour through a Chrysler factory.

CADILLAC MODEL 30

Cadillac made news headlines in 1908 with the announcement that it was replacing all of its lines with the Model 30. Available as a roadster, convertible, and four- and five-passenger touring cars, sales of this attractive new line were tremendous, overtaking all Cadillac sales records. The 1912 Model 30, shown here, was revolutionary – it was the first production car to offer the electric starting and ignition systems that are the foundation of what we use today.

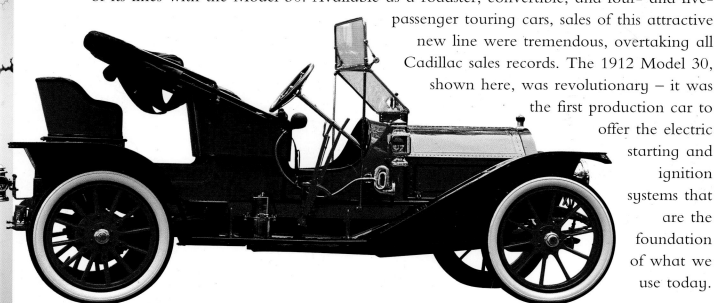

CADILLAC V-63

In 1924, Cadillac introduced a new design with a V8 engine – its most powerful motor to date. Known as the V-63 (right), Cadillac's latest creation was a luxurious five-passenger coupé. Over 19,000 were built and Cadillac retained its reputation as 'the standard of the world'. Back then, a well-used Model T Ford could be bought for just US$20, while a new Cadillac (depending on the model) fetched up to US$5000!

BMW DIXI

The Bayerisch Motoren Werke (Bavarian Motor Company) formed in 1916 with the merger of an aircraft maker and a manufacturer of aircraft engines. After World War I, though, the Versailles Treaty would not allow German companies to produce aircraft, so BMW turned their skills to the growing motorcycle market. Naturally, the next step was the motor car. In 1928 the company bought a factory that was producing a version of the English Austin Seven. This economy car became BMW's first automobile – Model 3/15, affectionately known as the 'Dixi'.

THE CLASSICS

Many classic cars today are worth more than they were when new, because they are much more difficult to find. The models shown here and on the following pages are just a few of the much-loved classics from days gone by. Each model has something special about it that makes people stop and say, "Now there goes a classic!"

HERE COME THE FINS...

After World War II, the American people were hungry for new and creative designs. As part of Cadillac's war involvement, a handful of executives were exposed to top-secret government projects. At one such viewing, a Cadillac designer spotted the Lockheed Lightning P-38 fighter plane, and was inspired by its vertical 'tailfins'. The first auto fins, although quite small, appeared on the 1948 Cadillac. The public loved them, and in the years that followed they continued to grow. By the mid 1950s, all the car manufacturers were developing their own versions – trying to 'out-fin' each other!

NO KEYS? NO PROBLEM!

A few classics, like the first E-type Jaguar produced in Britain in 1961, didn't require a key to start the engine. You could simply press a button and go!

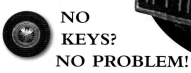

HOW MUCH MIGHT MY CLASSIC COST TODAY?

 Volkswagen Beetle (1957) £2500-7000

 Cadillac Sedan De Ville (1956) £2800-8000

Austin-Healey Sprite (1958) £2800-8400

Rolls Royce Silver Spirit MkI (1989) £13,400-24,500

Chevrolet Corvette Roadster (1962) £14,000-31,500

E-Type Jaguar XKE (1963) £12,500-38,500

Mercedes-Benz 300SL (1954) £48,950-154,000

Note: Figures are estimates only and will vary depending on condition and region.

UP TO:	£10,000	£20,000	£30,000	£40,000	£50,000 and more!

'THE BEST CAR IN THE WORLD'

Rolls Royce's classic Camargue (1975-86) earned this title because of its fine quality. Its ghostly quietness and shiny body also earned it the nickname 'Silver Ghost'.

BIG CAR, BIG TANK

Heavy duty petrol-guzzlers like the 1956 Cadillac Sedan de Ville, shown above, consumed petrol at a staggering rate of around 30 litres per 100 kilometres (6.5 gallons per 62 miles)!

CADILLAC SEDAN DE VILLE

The mid 1950s and '60s will be remembered for some of the biggest, boldest cars ever, particularly in the USA. As fast as one company produced a flashy new model, a rival quickly brought out an even more outrageous one. Despite many contenders during this era, Cadillac remained the USA's luxury sales leader. Others happily sold 40,000 cars a year – that was an average quarterly output for Cadillac!

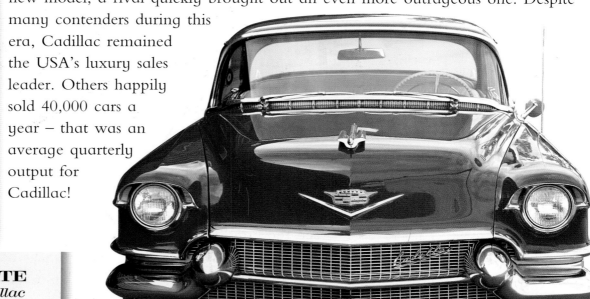

MEGA DATE
In 1956 Cadillac introduced their first hardtop Sedan de Ville (shown right).

ROLLS ROYCE SILVER SPIRIT

Britain's Rolls Royce made their first car in 1906 and they're still going strong, supplying top-quality cars for customers worldwide. One of the most luxurious models was the Silver Spirit Mark I (left), produced in 1980–89. The interior was dominated by a traditional wooden dashboard, with a choice of fine leather or velour upholstery.

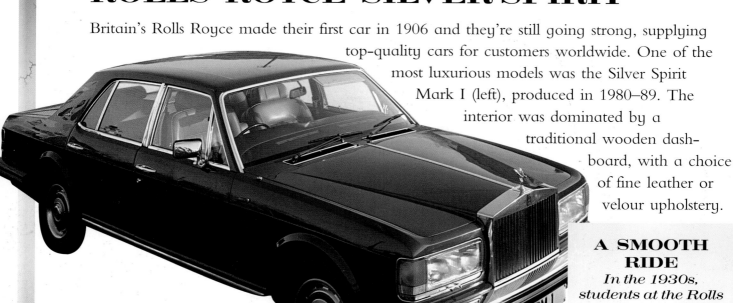

A SMOOTH RIDE
In the 1930s, students at the Rolls Royce school for chauffeurs had to drive with a glass of water balanced on the radiator — without spilling it.

MERCEDES-BENZ 300SL 'GULLWING'

This high-performance car remains one of the most desirable models of all time! The 1954 300SL has a huge 3.0 litre fuel-injected engine capable of reaching a top speed of 224 km/h (140 mph). As with many sports cars of the 1950s, there was little difference between road and racing versions. The most distinctive feature of the 300SL was the 'Gullwing' doors. When open, these upswinging doors looked just like a seagull's wings! They were vital because of the car's high seals – normal doors would have been impossible to open! Production of the 'Gullwing' ended in 1957 – in total, only 1400 models had been built.

INTERNET LINK
http://vintagecars.about.com
A great website directory that will help you find almost anything. Search the vintage cars section by country and make.

AUSTIN-HEALEY SPRITE

Austin-Healey introduced the Sprite in Britain in 1958. This small and zippy sports car quickly became popular, especially with younger drivers. Because of the unusual position of the headlights high up on the body, the first version of this model was nicknamed 'Frog-Eyed Sprite'. The Mark II edition was launched in 1962, this time with the headlights in a more conventional position.

HANDLE THIS!
The Austin Sprite had no external door handles! To open a door, you had to raise the soft top, reach over the window and pull the handles inside!

OLF 852E

E-TYPE JAGUAR

INTERNET LINK
http://www.javelinamx.com/carstars
Check out the original Batmobile and other top cars from classic films and TV shows like 'Charlie's Angels' and 'Starsky & Hutch'.

Unlike other supercars of its time, the E-type, or XKE, was produced for the mass-market and over 70,000 were built. Launched in 1961, following the success of the C- and D-types, this popular British sports car with a 3.8 litre 6-cylinder engine could reach speeds of almost 240 km/h (150 mph). In 1969, the series 11 E-types boasted several revisions, including a collapsible steering column – and the famous Jaguar starter button on the dashboard was replaced by the standard key start.

MEGA COOL
The 1963 E-Type Jaguar Series 1 Roadster, shown left, was the most fashionable car of its time.

CHEVROLET CORVETTE

The Chevy Corvette first appeared in 1953 as an American entry into the sports car market, which at one time was dominated by European makes. The second generation Corvette, with its fuel-injection engine, was launched in 1963. This model (right) even had a racing version, the Z-06. Luxury options such as power steering, air conditioning and leather seats were also available for the first time on these models. By 1968 the Corvette had changed dramatically in appearance and now had hidden windshield wipers and removable T-tops on coupé models.

VOLKSWAGEN BEETLE

Production of the classic VW Beetle began in 1940, but the factory was forced to close in 1944 due to World War II. After the war production resumed, but as materials were in short supply these early models were very primitive. (The interiors were stuck together with a fish-based glue, which gave off a dreadful smell!) In the 1960s the Beetle became most popular, and even gained cult status, when hippies considered it a symbol of peace.

MEGA FACT
The Volkswagen Beetle, with sales exceeding 20 million since the 1940s, holds the record for history's longest production run.

AAAHH...
When the VW Beetle was first manufactured, many people said it wouldn't sell — they thought it was too ugly!

POWER TRIP

Muscle cars and monster trucks are made to be big, powerful, reliable and most of all, exciting! Introduced in the 1960s, the first muscle cars were fast, 'tyre-smoking', relatively cheap – and designed to be noticed. With no thought for their heavy fuel consumption, these 'power cars' left others eating their dust. Then, in the 1970s, a number of American enthusiasts decided to 'muscle-up' their pick-up trucks, and so the monster truck was born.

Most muscle cars have a V6 or a massive V8 engine – like this one from a Chevy 502

MEGA MUSCLE
The world's fastest muscle car is the 1966 Cobra. But with a top speed of only 190 km/h (118 mph), it's no match for the McLaren F1!

FORD MUSTANG

The Ford Mustang began life in 1964, and quickly topped the sales charts. More than 100,000 were sold during its first four months on the market, making it Ford's most successful car since the Model T. Considered one of the first 'muscle' cars, the Mustang quickly caught the attention of the young, who rushed out in droves to buy one. Its popular features included excellent handling, a powerful engine and a flash, distinctive design. More than 30 years after the first model went on show, new Mustangs are still selling. But the original will always be a hard act to follow!

What is... FOUR-WHEEL DRIVE?

When all four wheels of a car are powered by the engine, it's called a four-wheel drive vehicle. So, if one wheel gets stuck, the others still function. Four-wheel drives are as reliable in mud or snow as they are on paved road. Historians are uncertain who invented the system, but the first 4WD vehicle was designed in 1900 by Ferdinand Porsche (yes, the founder of Porsche cars) for an Austrian truck manufacturer. The vehicle had electric hub motors on each wheel – powered by a generator. By the way, NASA used the idea of electric wheel hub motors to put its lunar vehicle in motion!

PLYMOUTH ROADRUNNER

In 1968, Plymouth decided that muscle cars had strayed too far from their original purpose, which was to be cheap, fast and exciting. So, they paid US$50,000 to Warner Bros to affix a cartoon bird onto a new vehicle, based on a Belvedere pillared coupé. With an ultimate speed of 154 km/h (96 mph), the Road Runner was born. Although it had numerous features, including beefed-up suspension and manual transmission, the interior was very basic. A horn that went 'beep-beep' was the finishing touch!

INTERNET LINKS

http://www.musclecars.net
Search for your favourite models and get technical information plus great photos.
http://www.thecarcollection.com
Find out the current value of your favourite car.

BIGFOOT

Bigfoot 1 was the first monster truck ever built, and is probably the most famous truck in the world. Starting life as a 1974 Ford F250 pick-up, Bigfoot was modified by its owner, who added bigger tyres and better suspension. Rear steering was included later. In 1981, Bigfoot began its 'car-crushing' career, performing in an American stadium. Various imitators followed, and car-crushing became a major event. By 1987 the latest-technology monster trucks were so fast, that they went from crushing other vehicles to racing them.

SPEED DEMONS

At the very top of the automotive pyramid sits the ultimate superstar – the exotic sports car. Amazingly fast and outrageously expensive, exotic production models don't need to be practical or cost-effective. With precision tuned, high-performance engines, these speed demons showcase the most advanced technologies a manufacturer has to offer.

WEIGHT CONSCIOUS

During the design of the McLaren F1, performance was the top priority, and the goal weight was set at 1000 kilograms (2204 lb). The final weight was 1140 kilograms (2513 lb) – still 40% lighter than a Lamborghini Diablo!

MCLAREN F40? When Gordon Murray designed the McLaren F1, he had a Ferrari F40 in the workshop to study its steering system as he considered the F40 to be the world's best handling car!

Ten of the FASTEST!

Model:	Approx. Maximum Speed:		0-97 km/h (60 mph):
McLaren F1	372 km/h	(231 mph)	3.2 seconds
Jaguar XJ220	349 km/h	(217 mph)	3.6
Lamborghini Diablo SE30	333 km/h	(208 mph)	4.0
Ferrari F40	324 km/h	(201 mph)	4.1
Ferrari 550 Maranello	320 km/h	(199 mph)	4.3
Porsche 959	315 km/h	(198 mph)	3.6
Porsche 911 GT2	315 km/h	(198 mph)	4.1
Ferrari 456M	299 km/h	(186 mph)	5.1
Lamborghini Countach QV5000s	293 km/h	(183 mph)	4.6
Aston Martin DB7 Vantage	290 km/h	(180 mph)	5.0

MCLAREN F1

The F1 was developed by McLaren Cars Ltd, and is the world's fastest, most expensive road car. And if you find a spare £600,000 at the bottom of your moneybox, there's no reason why you can't buy one! With its 6-speed manual gear transmission, the F1 has a powerful V12 BMW engine that can reach 97 km/h (60 mph) in 3.2 seconds! No other road car accelerates as fast, or has a maximum speed of over 372 km/h (231 mph). There is hardly a component in the F1 that has not been specially designed for it, mostly to save weight – the lighter the car, the faster it goes!

MEGA PEDAL
The accelerator pedal of the F1 is made up of six different titanium components alone.

FERRARI F40

Ferrari produced the F40 between 1987 and 1992, as a special supercar to celebrate the company's 40th anniversary. Early models boasted sliding windows, while the last F40s had wind-down windows and adjustable suspension. The body is made of carbon fibre so it will not rust, although it must be stored in a warm dry climate. If you look closely at the bodywork of an original F40 you should see the honeycomb weave underneath the paint. If you can't see the weave, then the car has been resprayed (some owners added an extra layer to create a perfectly smooth body).

MEGA FACT
All Ferrari F40s left the factory in red. Any other colour you might see is a respray, although many are factory official.

LAMBORGHINI COUNTACH

The name Lamborghini has always been linked with quality and a tradition of excellence – no matter what the product! The original owner of the company, Ferrucio Lamborghini, started out manufacturing tractors. Today, although best known for high-performance sports cars, the bull trademark represents a massive conglomerate of businesses that produces everything from air-conditioning systems to fashion accessories and golf carts! One of the most popular sports car models, the sleek Countach QV5000S (below), became available in 1986 with a top speed of 293 km/h (183 mph).

PORSCHE 911

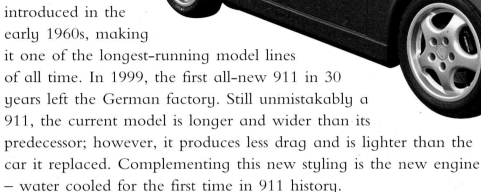

One of the few remaining icons of the auto world, the Porsche 911 was introduced in the early 1960s, making it one of the longest-running model lines of all time. In 1999, the first all-new 911 in 30 years left the German factory. Still unmistakably a 911, the current model is longer and wider than its predecessor; however, it produces less drag and is lighter than the car it replaced. Complementing this new styling is the new engine – water cooled for the first time in 911 history.

INTERNET LINKS

http://www.fantasycars.com
Get profiles on all luxury makes, and stay ahead of the game by discovering models yet to be released. There are fantastic screensavers to download too. See also:
http://www.ferrari.it
http://www.porsche.com
http://www.lamborghini.com

ASTON MARTIN DB7 VANTAGE

The Aston Martin marque represents the ultimate in 'civilised' high-performance sports cars, combining traditional British styling with the latest automotive technology. From the DB2 to the racing successes of DBR1 and James Bond's DB5, these are the best-known images of Aston Martin. The latest Vantage builds on the DB7, the most successful model in the history of the British automaker. The first Aston Martin with a 12-cylinder engine, it can reach 0-97 km/h (60 mph) within 5 seconds; top speed is 290 km/h (180 mph).

MEGA NAME
The DB of the famous Aston Martin range comes from the initials of former owner Sir David Brown, who bought the company in 1947. The most famous remains the DB5 – James Bond's car from the 1960s.

MEGA MILES
While developing the DB7 Vantage, Aston Martin made 30 prototype vehicles which covered 500,000 testing miles.

TRACK STARS

Racing cars on road-like tracks began in 1906. Since then, many different categories of professional motor racing have developed. Today we have Formula One, American Indy car, stock-car, drag, karting and rally driving, among others. Formula One is the most popular class outside the USA, where Indy car racing is the top event.

Racing cars go so fast that sometimes they almost take off! Aerofoils act like upside-down wings, keeping the tyres on the ground.

A streamlined body made of light materials increases speed by allowing air to pass over it easily.

The Grand Prix

Grand Prix is a series of motor races held to determine the world champion driver in Formula One racing (or, more formally, the World Championship of Drivers). More than 15 Grand Prix races are held yearly in countries throughout the world. The races are controlled by automobile manufacturers under the supervision of the FIA (Fédération Internationale de l'Automobile / International Automobile Federation), which sets the specifications for all racing-car classes.

RALLY DRIVING

Rally driving, which began in 1907, is a race whereby drivers follow a specified public route. The driver is accompanied by a navigator, and together they attempt to keep to a predetermined schedule between checkpoints. The longest rally race ever run was from London, England to Sydney, Australia, a distance of 31,107 kilometres (19,329 miles)!

FORMULA ONE V. INDY CAR

Formula One and Indy racing are for open-wheeled, single-seater cars with 6-speed transmissions and a V-8 or V-6 turbocharged engine placed behind the driver. Although the cars look very similar, there are some important differences:

- Indy cars begin races at race speed; Formula Ones begin from a dead stop.
- Formula One cars weigh 30% less than Indy cars.
- Formula One cars never race on oval tracks; Indy cars only race on oval tracks.

The fan pulls out air from under the car. This holds the car down on the track and helps it to go around corners faster.

Super wide tyres called 'slicks' give extra speed. The four grooves were introduced to slow the cars down!

MOLTO FERRARI!

Ferrari's competition record is amazing: eight victories at Le Mans between 1954–65, and nine World Championships. No other company has such a long history in racing, and while others rely on mainstream manufacturers for their engines and gearboxes, Ferrari rely on only one company. You guessed it — Ferrari!

MCLAREN F1

McLaren can boast over 130 Grand Prix victories since they started competing in 1968. The team holds the record for the most Grand Prix wins in a season, with Ayrton Senna and Alain Prost winning 15 out of 16 races in 1988! This McLaren Mercedes racer was a winner for David Coulthard in Brazil 2001.

INTERNET LINKS

http://www.formula1.com
Get the low-down on all Formula 1 events and the latest results.
http://www.f1-live.com
Exciting live coverage of Formula 1 racing, along with photos and screensavers to download.

DODGE VIPER

Unveiled in 1992, the original Dodge Viper roadster, with its muscular bodywork and enormous V10 engine, could do speeds of up to 269 km/h (168 mph). Its huge 415 horsepower engine allowed the Viper to run 0-97 km/h (60 mph) in 4.8 seconds. The more recent Viper Venom 600 GTS, with its 6-speed manual transmission, had even more bulges and spoilers added to it. A turbo engine to increase the power output to 602 bhp means that the 600 GTS can reach an incredible top speed of 325 km/h (203 mph)!

MEGA VIPER
The 1998 Dodge Viper, shown here, was the class winner of the 24-hour race at that year's Le Mans.

INDY 500

Dating back to 1911, the Indianapolis 500 is one of the oldest and most prestigious races in the world, taking place each year in May in Indiana, USA. Thirty-three drivers compete, each with a crew to support them. They spend three weeks in practice and qualifying runs to race for 805 kilometres (500 miles / 200 laps). The cars typically travel about 120 kilometres (75 miles) between pit stops, when they refuel and usually have the tyres changed.

RALLY CARS

Peugeot is one of the top names in the rally world, producing designs that are often adopted later by many of their competitors. These neat

MEGA 500
The fastest Indianapolis 500 occurred in 1990, when Dutch driver Arie Luyendyk completed the race at an average speed of 299 km/h (186 mph) in 2 hours 41 minutes 18.404 seconds.

and nifty cars (such as the 305 model, above) have won a number of World Rally Championships over the years for both driver and constructor. Another well-known rally car manufacturer is Audi, whose Quattro is one of the most important rally models of all time. Having made its introduction in 1980, the Quattro was the first car to take advantage of the new rules allowing four-wheel drive for rally competition.

ODDBALLS

These are just a few of history's weirdest, wackiest production models, from the tiny three-wheeled bubble car to the amphicar, which can carry you over both land and water!

SINCLAIR C5

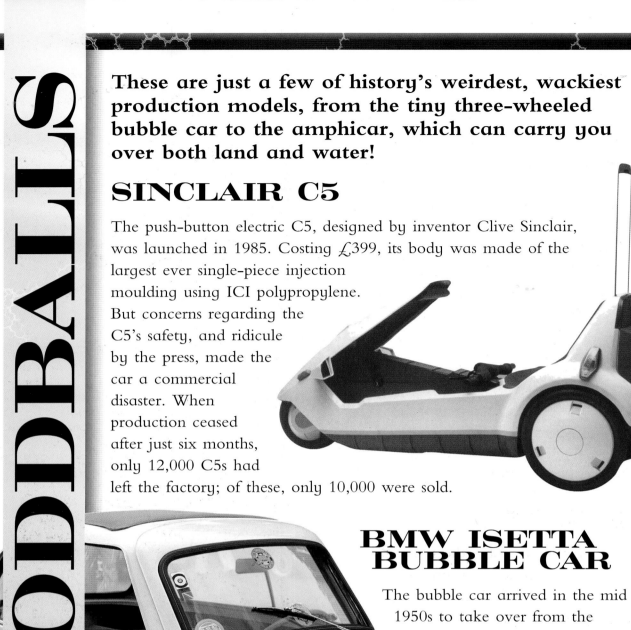

The push-button electric C5, designed by inventor Clive Sinclair, was launched in 1985. Costing £399, its body was made of the largest ever single-piece injection moulding using ICI polypropylene. But concerns regarding the C5's safety, and ridicule by the press, made the car a commercial disaster. When production ceased after just six months, only 12,000 C5s had left the factory; of these, only 10,000 were sold.

BMW ISETTA BUBBLE CAR

The bubble car arrived in the mid 1950s to take over from the motorcycle. The two main types were the Isetta and the Messerschmitt, both from Germany. These odd-looking 'bugs' could be seen everywhere, careering round corners on their three little wheels. The best news – you could drive approximately 101 kilometres (63 miles) on just 4.5 litres (one gallon) of petrol!

MEGA SPEED
The Isetta has a top speed of 80 km/h (50 mph) – providing it's travelling downhill, of course!

AMPHICAR

The amphibious car or 'amphicar', as it was known, was produced by the Amphicar Corporation in Germany between 1961 and 1968. It's estimated that only some 3700 were made, most of which were sold to the USA. Made of thick, old-fashioned steel, this 'oddball' was assembled with continuous welds and lead filling around the joins to make it completely watertight; the two doors were edged with rubber stripping. The amphicar moves in water with the use of twin nylon propellers. It can travel up to 11 km/h (7 mph) in water, and up to 112 km/h (70 mph) on land with a high-performance engine.

INTERNET LINK
www.amphicar.com
Explore the world of the amazing amphicar at the site of the official owners' club. Get the facts about its history and view some great action photos.

PEEL P50

The Peel P50 is probably the smallest motor car ever manufactured to carry an adult passenger. Constructed by the Peel Engineering Company on the Isle of Man, England, in 1962, it measures an amazing 1.34 metres (53 inches) in length, 99 centimetres (39 inches) in width – and just 1.34 metres (53 inches) in height! And with a weight of only 59 kilograms (132 lb), you could always put it on the back of a toy truck and pull your Peel home if it broke down!

MEGA LIMO
One of the most outrageous cars ever is an American limousine. With 26 wheels, it's over 30 metres (98 feet) long. It has a swimming pool and a helicopter landing pad. When turning, it simply bends in the middle!

FUTURE FEATURES

Cars are changing, and for many reasons. Fuel shortages, dirty air, global warming – all of these factors have brought tougher government controls to the car industry. But manufacturers are already making amazing progress. Today's advances will result in cars that give fewer emissions, go farther on less fuel – and run as quiet as a mouse!

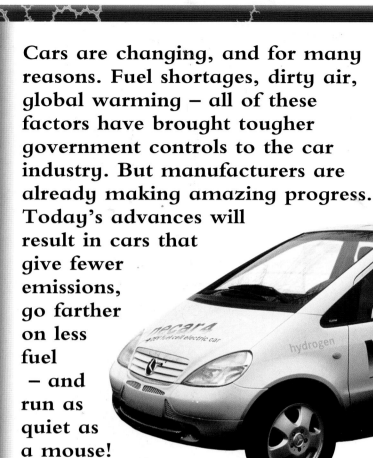

DAIMLER-BENZ F300 LIFE-JET

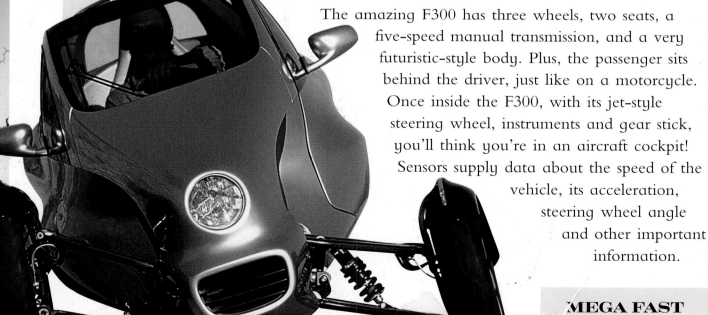

The amazing F300 has three wheels, two seats, a five-speed manual transmission, and a very futuristic-style body. Plus, the passenger sits behind the driver, just like on a motorcycle. Once inside the F300, with its jet-style steering wheel, instruments and gear stick, you'll think you're in an aircraft cockpit! Sensors supply data about the speed of the vehicle, its acceleration, steering wheel angle and other important information.

Nutty way to fuel your car!

Fuel cell-driven cars of the future could be powered by hazelnuts! Sounds nutty? Well... it's thought that hazelnuts could produce the hydrogen needed to generate an electric current for electric and hybrid cars. This is great news for Turkey, the world's largest producer of hazelnuts. The annual hazelnut harvest from this country alone could produce enough hydrogen for 2000 cars to each travel up to 76,000 kilometres (10,000 miles)!

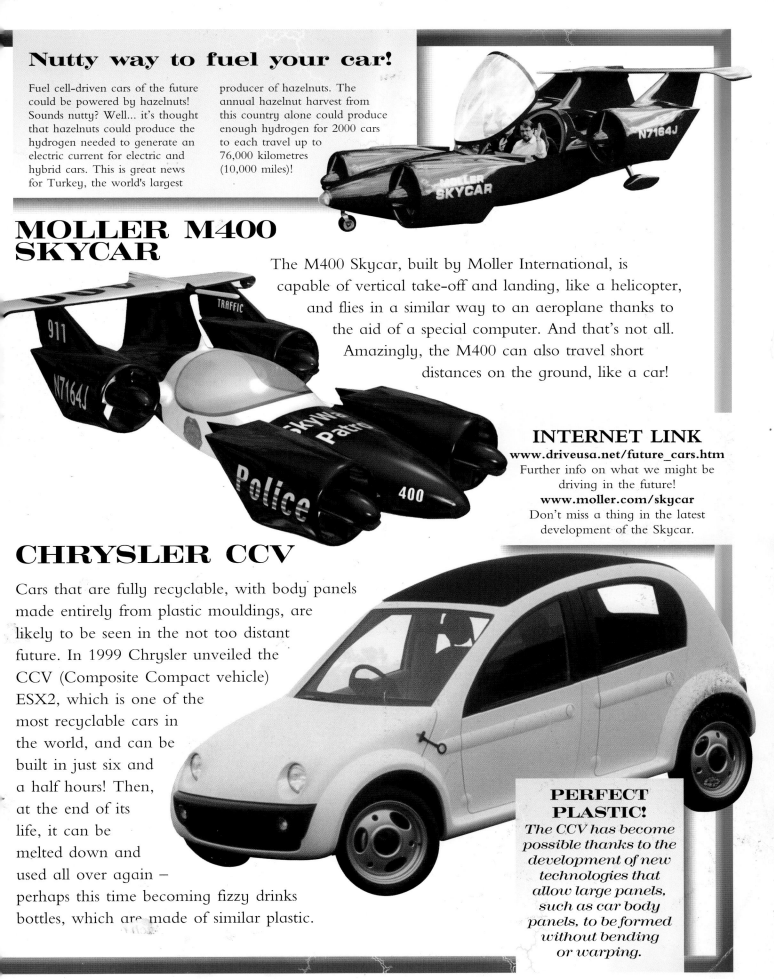

MOLLER M400 SKYCAR

The M400 Skycar, built by Moller International, is capable of vertical take-off and landing, like a helicopter, and flies in a similar way to an aeroplane thanks to the aid of a special computer. And that's not all. Amazingly, the M400 can also travel short distances on the ground, like a car!

INTERNET LINK

www.driveusa.net/future_cars.htm
Further info on what we might be driving in the future!
www.moller.com/skycar
Don't miss a thing in the latest development of the Skycar.

CHRYSLER CCV

Cars that are fully recyclable, with body panels made entirely from plastic mouldings, are likely to be seen in the not too distant future. In 1999 Chrysler unveiled the CCV (Composite Compact vehicle) ESX2, which is one of the most recyclable cars in the world, and can be built in just six and a half hours! Then, at the end of its life, it can be melted down and used all over again – perhaps this time becoming fizzy drinks bottles, which are made of similar plastic.

PERFECT PLASTIC!

The CCV has become possible thanks to the development of new technologies that allow large panels, such as car body panels, to be formed without bending or warping.

GLOSSARY

BHP Brake Horsepower, a measurement of the engine's maximum power output. (The Lamborghini Countach shown here has the same power as 455 horses coming from its engine!)

CARBURETTOR An instrument that mixes fuel and air into a combustible vapour. (The European Countach has six twin-choke carburettors – most cars have one!)

MEGA CARS
Although they look totally different, the VW Beetle on page four and the Lamborghini Countach below use the same basic manufacturing concepts and components.

FUEL INJECTION An electronic system that monitors engine conditions and provides the correct air/fuel mixture based on the engine's demand. This eliminates the need for a carburettor.

US SPEC
New cars bound for the USA must meet US specifications, or 'US spec'. Namely, they must have a fuel-injected engine which produces fewer emissions and is therefore less harmful to the environment.

CHASSIS
The structural frame upon which a vehicle is built.

CLUTCH A device that connects the wheels to the engine, enabling the gears to be changed.

COUPE A two-door, hard-top passenger car that seats up to four or five people.

IGNITION
An electrical system that produces a spark to ignite the fuel/air mixture in a petrol engine.

MARQUE The brand name of a car manufacturer. Rolls Royce, Ford, Chevrolet and Lamborghini are just a few well-known marques.

POWER STEERING Makes the steering wheel move more easily than a manual steering system.

ROADSTER An open-top car, especially one seating only one or two people.

RPM Revolutions Per Minute, a unit of measure used to express the rotational speed of an engine. (The Countach will spin at up to 7000 rpm!)

SHOCK ABSORBER A hydraulic suspension component that absorbs energy 'shock' and so contributes to a smoother, more controlled ride. (The Countach has two for each of its huge rear wheels!)

TORQUE The amount of force supplied by an engine. (The European Countach has a maximum torque of 369 lb ft @ 5200 rpm.)

TRANSMISSION A mechanism (that includes the gears) linking the power produced by the engine to the drive wheels.

CAR CRAZY
There are a staggering 200 million cars in the USA today — that's 40% of the world's total!

CAR TOWN
Car manufacturing is a major industry the world over. Some factories are as big as an average town, with thousands of employees.

TURBOCHARGER
A compressor which boosts the engine's intake pressure. In low gears, more torque is delivered to the wheels, improving the car's road-holding ability.

INDEX

Motoring Magazines:

- ✗ Autocar
- ✗ AutoExpress
- ✗ Autosport
- ✗ BBC Top Gear
- ✗ Car Magazine
- ✗ Classic & Sports Car
- ✗ Classic Car Weekly
- ✗ Classic Motor Monthly
- ✗ F1 Racing
- ✗ Land Rover World
- ✗ Off Road & 4 Wheel Drive
- ✗ Thoroughbred & Classic Cars
- ✗ What Car?

Picture Credits

T=top; B=bottom; C=centre
8T Phil Talbot/Auto Express; 15T CD Photo Library; 16B CD Photo Library; 17T Phil Talbot; 17B Phil Talbot/Auto Express; 18 Auto Express; 19 Auto Express; 21B Auto Express; 22 Formula One Pictures; 23 Formula One Pictures; 24T Formula One Pictures; 25T Empics; 25B Empics; 26T Sinclair/Patric Baird; 27T David Chapman; 27C David Chapman; 28T Daimler-Benz; 28B Daimler-Benz; 29T Moller International; 29C Moller International; 29B Chrysler/Car & Truck News

All other pictures Chrysalis Images